Copyright © 2025 Exaltation Press

Author: Larisa Faberova
Illustrator: Ekaterina Zavalova
Translator: Fr. John Hogg
Editor: Sally Boyle

"The Life of the Holy Great-martyr Catherine"
This book is part of the series "Lives of Saints for Children." In this book, children will learn about the life of the holy Great-martyr Catherine of Alexandria, and the importance of loving Christ with a pure heart and standing firm in the truth, even when it means great sacrifice.

All rights reserved. This book or any portion thereof may not be reproduced or used in any manner whatsoever without the express written permission of the publisher except for the use of brief quotations in a book review.

Translated from the original "Житие святого Великомученицы Екатерины в пересказе для детей" by Nikea Press, Copyright © Trading House «NIKEA», www.Nikeabooks.ru

ISBN: 978-1-950067-96-1 (Hardcover)
    978-1-950067-95-4 (Paperback)

First printing edition 2025

Exaltation Press
Grand Rapids, MI

www.ExaltationPress.com

For bulk orders, please contact editor@exaltationpress.com

Help us build our permanent temple for future generations! Scan this QR-code to donate to Holy Cross Antiochian Orthodox Church in Grand Rapids, MI. Thank you and God bless you!

Larisa Faberova

The Life of the Holy Great-martyr Catherine
Retold for Children

Illustrations by

Ekaterina Zavalova

Grand Rapids · Exaltation Press · 2024

The Lord, in His great love for each of us, gives each person certain talents. Sometimes, He gives us talents that fit with the meaning of our name. For example, Andrew means "courageous," so someone with that name might be blessed with the gift of being courageous. Someone named Michael might be righteous and just. Arseny, whose name means "virile" or "manly," would be fearless and reliable. Someone named Natalia would treat everyone like they were family. Anastasia might help to restore or resurrect (as the name means in Greek) people's faith in God. Eugene or Eugenia would do good works. But what talent might the Lord give to someone named Catherine? Catherine means "clean," so He would likely give her the difficult gift of purity—purity of heart, soul, mind, and body. Why is this gift difficult? Because in order to receive this gift you would have to spend your whole life, every day and every minute, fighting against yourself, your passions, and your own selfishness.

Almost three hundred years after the birth of Christ in the city of Alexandria in Egypt, a daughter was born to the city's ruler. She was a true princess, and she was given the name Catherine.

In those days, girls weren't given any

education. Women took care of the home, raised children, and cooked the food, but they often weren't able to read or write or count. Princesses were no exception. Of course, girls were taught some things—how to sew, knit, dance, and draw. Princesses were also taught good manners, how to dine properly and elegantly at the royal table with guests, and how to make light conversation with those who were invited to a reception. Princess Catherine was an obedient girl, and she learned everything that a girl of a royal family was supposed to.

Catherine was twelve years old when she felt a desire to learn more. One day, she went and asked her mother to hire teachers to come to the palace to teach her—only the best teachers of philosophy, the Greek language and literature, math, and public speaking. Her mother wasn't surprised. She had seen her daughter's talent for learning.

Catherine's teachers were overjoyed

with her progress! She was such a dedicated and interested student that she mastered the difficult subjects and foreign languages better than any of their other students, even though they were all boys or even grown men.

The city of Alexandria was one of the capital cities of the enormous Roman Empire. It contained one of the most important centers of learning of the whole ancient world—the Library of Alexandria. Princess Catherine loved to go there and unroll and read the scrolls in the library. (This was

before the time of books.) As she read the scrolls, ancient history came alive to her, and the secrets of medicine, science, and philosophy opened up before her. Catherine also knew many languages and often helped ambassadors from distant lands conduct negotiations at court.

Everyone who saw her was struck not only by her uncommon beauty but also by the uncommon extent of her learning. Many princes wanted to marry Catherine, but none of them were her equal in intelligence and education. Her relatives tried to convince her to find a husband that would allow her family to make alliances with other countries, but marrying someone just for political reasons, without love, would have forever tainted the purity of her heart, soul, and body. Catherine thought to herself, "A person's true riches and beauty are in his heart. He should have a heart that is pure, kind, sincere, and diligent. Beauty doesn't last forever. It disappears when old age or illness come."

She told her mother, the queen, "I will only marry a man who is my equal in knowledge, wealth, beauty, and wisdom." This saddened her mother because she knew her daughter's strength of character and determination.

During the time of Catherine, in the third century, there were Christians everywhere in the Roman Empire. The impious Emperor Maximinus hated the Christians, and he began cruelly persecuting them. If they refused to offer sacrifices to the pagan gods, they were subjected to horrible torments, thrown into cages, fed to hungry lions, or drowned in the sea.

Catherine's mother, the queen, was secretly a Christian. She decided to take Catherine to see her spiritual father, a righteous elder, and ask for his advice.

The queen and Princess Catherine packed secretly and set out to see the elder. He lived in a remote desert place, in a cave where he had built a small monastic cell and a church. When the elder met Catherine and saw her beauty, intelligence, purity, and humility, he decided to tell her

about Christ, the King of Heaven.

"I know one Man," the elder said, "who exceeds you in all of your gifts. You are beautiful, but his beauty is brighter than the sunlight. You are smart, but his wisdom governs the whole world. You are wealthy, but the whole world belongs to Him. You are a princess, but He is the great, unfathomable King of both heaven and earth."

As she listened to the elder, Catherine thought that he was talking about some king that she had never heard about. She was surprised at what she was hearing, so she asked, "Is what you're telling me the truth? Whose son is this man?"

"He has no earthly father," the elder answered, "and He was born in an inexplicable way from an All-holy and All-pure Virgin. She has been raised higher than the heavens, where all the angels glorify her as the Queen of Heaven."

"May I see this young man?" Catherine asked, her heart beating in her chest.

The elder was silent for a moment and then said, "If you do what I ask you to do, you will see his bright face."

"You are a respected elder. I believe that you are telling me the truth. I will be a good student," Catherine whispered, "and I am ready to do whatever you tell me so that I may see him."

The elder gave her an icon of the Most-holy Theotokos with her Divine Son in her arms. "This is an image of the mother of the One that I told you so many wondrous things about. Take this icon with you to the palace. Close your door and pray with reverence to this Virgin—her name is Mary. Ask her to show you her Son. If you ask her with faith and hope, she will hear you and allow you to see Who it is that your soul is longing for."

When she got home, the princess closed the door of her room, lit a candle in front of the icon, and began to pray like the elder had instructed her, hoping that her requests would be miraculously fulfilled by the Virgin Mary. Time passed, and Catherine got tired and fell asleep. Then, she suddenly saw the Heavenly Queen! She looked just as she did in the icon, holding her Child, who shone brighter than the sun. Catherine couldn't see His face, however, because He had His head turned and was looking at the Theotokos. The princess went around to the Theotokos' other side, her heart trembling, but the Child again turned away from her. Three times, Catherine walked around the Theotokos and her Child until finally, the Mother of God spoke to her Son, saying, "Look, my Son, at your handmaiden Catherine! Look at how splendid and good she is!"

The Christ Child, however, responded, "No, this maiden is so disfigured that I cannot even look at her! Have her go back to the elder who gave her the icon and do everything that he tells her. Then she shall see Me."

Princess Catherine awoke from her dream. Just a moment before, it had been a bright, sunny day. The divine Child was there in front of her, shining brighter than the sun! A moment before, the purest of all women, the Most-pure Theotokos, was there speaking kindly about Catherine, who herself loved purity! Now, the room was dark. The moonlight was streaming through the window, and the candle had gone out. Looking at the icon, it seemed to Catherine that the Theotokos was looking right at her, lovingly.

As soon as she felt the warmth of the sunrise, Catherine set off alone to see the elder. She went alone, not wanting to endanger anyone, since it was such a horrible time of persecution for Christians. Catherine had always trusted her teachers, starting with the tutors that came to teach her at the palace and then later those great teachers that she got to know by reading their writings in the scrolls in the library. Now, she could feel that Someone that loved her was giving her the most important teacher she'd ever have—the righteous elder. She sensed this would be the most important lesson of her entire life.

When she entered the elder's cell, the princess fell to her knees before him and, with tears in her eyes, told him what had happened the night before. With his spiritual eyes, the elder could see that this beautiful, rich, and wise princess kneeling in front of him was ready for something greater. She was ready to become a Christian. He could see that she already loved the Lord Jesus Christ with a pure love. So the elder began to teach her the mysteries of the Christian faith. He taught her sacred history—from the creation of the world and of mankind, to the expulsion of Adam and Eve from paradise, to the coming of Christ the Savior.

When the elder told her about the Nativity of Christ, Catherine could suddenly see the whole scene—the manger, the donkey and sheep, the shepherds and the Magi—all of them had come to worship the Child. When he told her about the wedding in Cana of Galilee, Catherine pictured herself sitting near the Theotokos watching as the Lord turned water into wine. In her mind, she went with the disciples as they followed the Savior, and she listened as He preached, standing among the people on the mount. Then, she wept without ceasing as she followed the crowd watching the bloodied Christ carry his cross. She shed even more tears as Christ was crucified. But the elder touched her shoulder.

"Don't weep. Rejoice! He rose again!"

This was the most important lesson of all, and Catherine took it in wholeheartedly.

She committed to memory all the Christian teachings the elder shared and believed in Jesus Christ with her whole heart. She was then baptized by the wise elder.

Princess Catherine now understood that faith and hope, purity and faithfulness, and firmness in heavenly love were her true path. The elder told her to pray once more to the Most-pure

Theotokos that night and ask to see her.

When Catherine left the elder, it was nighttime. She walked through the sleepy city, listening to her heart. She had become a Christian! She now knew God! For her, the endless starry sky above her and the wide world spread out before her under the sky were both filled with the Kingdom of God. And she, the handmaid of God Catherine, belonged to the King of Heaven and to no one else! She would give the Lord her most precious treasure—a heart that was pure and loving. And she would give Him all of it.

Back at the palace, Catherine lit a candle in front of the icon and got on her knees and began to pray. Tears poured from her eyes as she asked the Mother of God to show herself again with her radiant Son and to show Catherine the new path that she should take in her new life as a Christian. She prayed all night until she fell asleep from exhaustion. Just then, she beheld the Queen of Heaven, the Most-holy Virgin, with her Divine Son in her arms! The light surrounding the Child in His mother's arms filled Catherine's entire room, as if the sun itself had entered her room. This time, the Child looked right at Catherine joyfully, with a smile on his face. The Theotokos asked Him, "And now, my Son, is this girl pleasing to you?"

"Yes," He replied, "very pleasing since now she is truly splendid and glorious, truly rich and wise. I love her so much that I want to betroth Myself to her as her Eternal Bridegroom."

The Most-holy Theotokos took Catherine's hand and said to her Son, "Give her an engagement ring. Make her your bride so that You can give her your Kingdom!" The Lord Jesus then gave Princess Catherine a ring that shone with his light. "Behold," He said, "I have chosen you as my eternal bride. Preserve the bond between us, guard your heart in purity, and seek no earthly bridegroom."

Catherine awoke, wiped the tears of joy from her eyes, and suddenly noticed an unusually beautiful ring on her hand! She felt such joy and thankfulness that, from that moment on, her heart was fully dedicated to God's divine love.

"Blessed are the pure in heart," Catherine said, remembering the elder's words, and her heart rejoiced. She would guard her purity of heart! She also remembered the words, "For where your treasure is, there your heart will be also." She asked herself, "Where was my treasure before? In the library. In the scrolls and tablets of clay with ancient texts from ancient writers and philosophers. My treasure was in knowing a lot about people, history, and medicine. I was like an ancient person with an ancient heart, but now, a new, heavenly knowledge has been revealed to me. My treasure is now in heaven, where my heart is as well!"

The wise princess prayed to Christ to teach her love and faithfulness. It didn't take long for her Heavenly Bridegroom to answer her request.

Not long after Catherine's baptism, Maximinus, the wicked emperor who was persecuting Christians throughout the whole Roman Empire, came to Alexandria on a visit. He decided to throw a triumphant feast in honor of the pagan gods, for all the people of the land. Notices were sent out throughout the empire, commanding people to come to Alexandria and offer sacrifices to the emperor's gods. A large assembly gathered for the feast, with some people bringing cows or sheep, while other poorer people brought geese, guinea fowl, or doves. The rich came bringing enormous herds. It was horribly noisy, with people shouting and the animals brought for sacrifice braying and crying. The smoke and stench of the sacrifices made it hard to breathe.

Catherine looked out her window at the scene and suddenly saw the people for who they were—a great crowd of people who were perishing because they did not know the Lord Jesus Christ. So, she put on her royal purple garments, left the palace, and went to the large pagan temple. When

she stood in the doorway, all eyes turned and looked at her because of the divine beauty that was shining in and through her. The princess then told Emperor Maximinus that she wanted to tell him something important. He told her to approach, so she came forward and made a bow, as was appropriate.

"O, emperor, look around!" she began, speaking in a loud voice. "Where is the god to whom you offer these bloody sacrifices? These statues of Zeus, Artemis, and Apollo are nothing but dwellings of demons! Remember how the great ancient philosophers laughed at them and sought the One True God!"

The emperor became angry listening to her because what she said went against all of his pagan beliefs. His face turned purple as the blood rushed to his face, but he controlled himself.

"Let us make our sacrifices during the days of this feast, and then I will listen to what you have to say," he said.

Later, when the emperor called Princess Catherine into his imperial chambers, he asked her to tell him who she was and to repeat what she had said to him before.

"I am a king's daughter," she answered, "and my name is Catherine. My whole life I have loved studying all the sciences. I have studied philosophy, literature, geometry, foreign languages, and medicine. But now, the Lord has revealed Himself to me, and I have become the bride of Christ! Now I measure all that I have learned by my faith in the Lord."

The emperor listened to Catherine and was surprised at her knowledge and intelligence. He was most struck, however, by her beauty. "Yes," he thought, "she must have been born from the gods. Such beauty cannot be human. She is a goddess!" Surprising even himself, he began to offer her half of his empire if she would renounce her Lord and offer sacrifices to Apollo.

"You will live with me, the emperor, and will live more happily than anyone has ever lived before!"

Catherine smiled and answered, "I will make you a different offer. My God is the God of Truth. You should turn to Him. "He is so powerful that if I only speak His name or trace the sign of the Cross in the air, your gods will fall from their pedestals and be shattered."

Although it was difficult for him to control himself, the emperor responded, "It is unbecoming for an emperor to speak to women. Nevertheless, I will gather my wisest philosophers to show you your error, and you will understand and will believe in our gods."

From all across the empire, intelligent and educated men answered the emperor's call. Fifty of the most well-known philosophers and orators gathered in Alexandria, all of them clever and

ንገተ ለአበር ሳውያም ዓሩ... ...
ዩችን ሲያደርጉ የቀዱቾ ዳኒል ኔፍስስ አባል እገሮ
ር ሴኔ ወር በቀሪበው ለደሉ ዩትበበር ማዕቀፍ ስምምነ
ኝንት ሁለት ሂሴ... ...ማዊል አምስት የለይኛ
ስ አባል ... ... ውስ ብራርማሸ
ታዎ
ከት   እና ሱዳ
ን   ወዱ ቪሆ
                                      ማማግ
                                      ግ ለበቂ
                                      ወላ ካለሳ
                                      ውልኸ
                                      አጀ ሴ
                                      ፔ ማንግ
                                      ግ በዚህ
                                      ሰ ያለሸ
                                      ማዌ የ
                                      ዳ ለስቱ
                                      ሸም ስለ
                                      ሸ ለ ሁ
                                      ስትሩ
                                      ፋሊ ለ
                                      ፋ ረ
                                      ግ ር ላ
                                      ከሁ
                                      ስ ስ
                                      ሰ ም

የደረስው ስምምነት ዞወረ ይለፍ
ጢቃዊ ... ...
ዚህ ስምምነት ከለቹው የተፋስስ
ፍለጥ ክማምክ የተለየ ጥቀ፤ ስለጋነጭ በለዴ...
ቸው ነዳ፤   በዓስማ የተሰፈ እ
አሁን ዓሬ   ሰ ለለለ አሉ በዚህ

eloquent. The emperor greeted them, saying:

"Use all your training to prepare yourselves for a debate. You must use your words to convince a certain girl to worship our gods. Don't think that it will be an easy debate just because your opponent will be a young maiden. I know that her wisdom is greater even than the great philosopher Plato. If you win the debate, I will reward you, but if you fail, you will be executed."

The wisest of the philosophers boldly answered the emperor:

"Do not be afraid, emperor. Our opponent may be wise, but she is a woman, which means that she cannot be the one who possesses the truth. Surely, when she sees fifty men as wise as we are, she will be ashamed and surrender."

When he heard the philosopher's confident and boastful words, the emperor calmed down and began to feel better, so he sent for Catherine.

Meanwhile, Catherine was on her knees, praying in front of her icon. A lamp was burning, and the princess was asking her Heavenly Bridegroom to test her love for Him. Just then, she heard a voice ringing out in her heart: "Rise and do not be afraid, O maiden of the Lord!" There in front of her stood the Archangel Michael. He shone with such radiant light that Catherine felt as though she were already in Heaven.

"I have been sent to you by your Bridegroom," the archangel said. "What you are doing is good. The Lord sees your love for Him. Soon, you will have to debate with the philosophers. Know that in addition to your own knowledge, the Lord will give you divine wisdom. But know, also, that you will receive a martyr's crown in the end and will bring many people to the Lord with you."

Just then, there was a knock at the door. They had come for Catherine. She looked around her room and saw that the candle in front of the icon had burned down, and it was dark.

The first philosopher who came to debate Catherine was the same one who had boasted in front of the emperor. When he saw her, he said, "So you are the one who dares to mock our gods so insolently?"

"I am," she answered humbly. "But it is not with impudence, but with humility and love for the truth, that I say your gods are nothing."

"Then tell me, girl, why the ancient scrolls don't say anything about this crucified Savior of yours?"

Catherine wasn't surprised by the question, but she was a little surprised when she heard herself answering him in a voice filled with joy. Without knowing it, she had been collecting the prophecies of the birth of the Christ Child that were in the ancient texts and treasuring them in her heart since she was young. Filled with wisdom, Catherine easily and joyfully told the philosopher these things that she had known before but hadn't understood and about the knowledge that she had been given according to the promise of the Archangel Michael.

As he listened to her, the philosopher who was debating her fell silent, his mouth open in amazement. She was citing many examples that he also knew from ancient manuscripts! And she quoted them as if reading from a scroll that only she could see! After this, the other wise men refused to debate her.

"If the wisest of us is silent and open-mouthed before her, what could we possibly say?"

Enraged, the emperor commanded that a large fire to be lit in the middle of the city and that all the philosophers and wise men be burned in the fire. They fell at Catherine's feet and asked her to pray for them to the True God, Whom they had come to love through her words. She said to them:

"You are blessed and happy because you

have left the darkness and have seen the True Light! You have renounced a mortal, earthly king and have come to the immortal King of Heaven! Believe firmly in His mercy!"

That evening after the fire, curious onlookers and Christians alike came to take pieces of the bones of the wise men who had been burned after believing in Christ. But,

they found the dead bodies completely intact, as if the fire had not even burned the hair of their heads! Seeing such a miracle, many in the crowd turned to Christ the Savior, and they buried the bodies of the martyrs with great reverence and honor.

The emperor, meanwhile, was becoming more and more angry. "My patience has come to an end!" he shouted at Princess Catherine. "Either you willingly offer sacrifices to Hermes, the god of learning (since he must be the one who gave you such talent!), or I will force you to do it!"

"Do as you wish," Catherine responded. "Suffering for the Lord is a sure path to Him," she said as she looked at her ring.

The emperor commanded that Catherine be stripped of her royal purple robe and that her bare body be mercilessly beaten with ropes that had knots tied in them. She was beaten for two hours, so severely that her back, chest, and stomach were covered with bloody wounds. However, St. Catherine only smiled and sang something, although nobody could hear what she was singing. In his rage at his inability to break her spirit, the emperor gave the command that she be shut up in the dungeon without food or water.

Princess Catherine, however, was not left without the care of her Heavenly Bridegroom. Every day that she stayed in the dungeon, a dove flew through the bars of the prison window, bringing her a small bundle of food and drink. Catherine waited, prayed, and had faith. And then, one day the Lord Jesus Christ Himself came to her with his angels and saints. The small prison seemed to open up as wide as the heavens, as though she were being lifted up to Heaven, rather than her Bridegroom coming down to her. "Do not be afraid, My beloved Bride. I am always with you," she heard in her

heart, "and no suffering shall overcome you! Your purity, patience, and courage will turn many to Me, and you shall receive the Kingdom of Heaven as your reward." When she was again alone in the prison, she glanced at her ring, and with all her strength she resolved that, no matter how painful or terrifying it might be, she would always preserve her union with God, her Bridegroom and Savior.

Around this time, one of the emperor's courtiers came to him and said that he had invented a torture device that would make Catherine renounce her God.

"Order your servants to build four wheels and put knives on those wheels. Then, tie the maiden in between the wheels. I'm certain, however, that as soon as Catherine sees them, she will change her mind and do whatever you ask."

The emperor liked this idea, and he

commanded the courtier to make this awful machine of death. When everything was ready, they brought Catherine out of her prison cell. The emperor walked up and looked closely at her, hoping to see fear and despair in her eyes, but he was shocked at what he saw instead! Catherine had just spent two weeks in prison without any food or drink (which he knew was the case, since the guards reported to him every day), and before she was imprisoned, she had been tortured so much that her body was one great wound. Now, however, she stood fearlessly before him, shining with an otherworldly beauty. Without fear or protest, she allowed herself to be tied to the machine, but as soon as it began to work, lightning struck the courtier who was turning the wheels. An angel from heaven then came down and first freed Catherine from the cords with which she was bound and then destroyed the wheel machine, scattering its pieces in every direction.

The emperor flew into a rage! He didn't see the angel or the lightning, and yet his courtier was dead, the machine had been shattered into pieces, killing his servant, and the princess was standing there, looking at him calmly, in all of her beauty. He couldn't understand what had happened! He hated her. He hated her God. Maximinus now understood that neither persuasion, nor flattery, nor promises of a happy life in the palace could make this holy virgin, with a will as unbreakable as diamond, renounce her faith. Maximinus decided right then what to do and commanded that her head be cut off with a sword.

The soldiers took Catherine, who was still completely calm, and led her outside the city walls. Many people, both men and women, walked along with Catherine and the soldiers, weeping that such a wise and beautiful young woman was about to be killed.

"Do not weep for me! Rejoice!" the holy Great-martyr Catherine said to them. "Now, I will see my beloved Bridegroom, Jesus Christ, my Savior! He is calling me to heavenly bliss. Weep for yourselves that you do not yet know the Lord!"

When they got to the place of execution, the holy great-martyr fell to her knees and began to pray, but no one could hear what she was saying. Sometimes, she raised her hands to her eyes, and when she did, her ring glistened in the sunlight. When she had finished praying, St. Catherine placed her head on the small marble column that had been placed there and said to the soldier: "Do what you have been ordered to."

The soldier then raised his sword and cut off Catherine's head.

The people watching had no time to wipe away their tears before six angels appeared and lifted the great-martyr's body and carried it to the highest peak of Mount Sinai.

Two hundred years later, a pilgrim appeared at the door of a monk's cell in a small monastery at the foot of Mt. Sinai. The pilgrim wore simple black monastic robes, but when he raised his arm just a little, you could see a bright angelic light shining from under his sleeve. The pilgrim said:

"At the top of the highest peak of Mt. Sinai lies the body of a great saint. Gather the monks, and I will show you the way."

With prayers and hymns, the monks followed their strange guide, who illuminated the road for them in a mysterious way. The path was long and difficult, but when they reached the end, they found the incorrupt relics of the holy Great-martyr Catherine. Her ring, a sign of the love of her heavenly Bridegroom, was still on her hand, and it was shining! The holy Great-martyr Catherine had been blessed with many talents, but she had used them all to glorify her Heavenly Bridegroom, Jesus Christ.

The life of this dear saint teaches us many things, but one of the things it shows us is the immense value of putting trust in the Lord. Do you see how important it is for each of us to trust the Lord in our own lives? God has given each of us life and has blessed us with various talents. Every day, He gives us food and cares for us. Why? Because He loves each of us. We should try to answer His love with our own love, with with purity of heart, and with hard work in service to our neighbors — because God loves each of them, too!

www.ingramcontent.com/pod-product-compliance
Lightning Source LLC
Chambersburg PA
CBHW052126070526
44586CB00016B/2102